New York's Land an[

Shaping the Growth of New [

Greg Roza

ROSEN CLASSROOM
PRIMARYSOURCE

Rosen Classroom Books & Materials

New York

Published in 2003 by The Rosen Publishing Group, Inc.
29 East 21st Street, New York, NY 10010

Book Design: Ron A. Churley

Photo Credits: Cover, p. 1 © Hulton-Deutsch Collection/Corbis; p. 4 © Smithsonian American Art Museum, Washington, D.C.; pp. 6, 16, 18 (both) © Corbis; p. 8 © Map Resources; p. 8 (inset) © Hulton/Archive; pp. 10, 12 © NorthWind Pictures; p. 14 © Museum of the City of New York/Corbis; p. 20 © Bettmann/Corbis.

ISBN: 0-8239-8411-7
6-pack ISBN: 0-8239-8423-0

Manufactured in the United States of America

Contents

The Beauty of New York 5

Native Americans of New York 7

Europeans Explore New York 9

Colonists and New York's Geography 11

From Beaver Furs to Farming 13

Colonial Buildings and Towns 15

Fighting Over New York 17

New York's Waterways 19

New York's Industry 21

New York Today 22

Glossary 23

Index 24

Primary Source List 24

Web Sites 24

4

The Beauty of New York

New York state has many beautiful sights. The Hudson River is the longest river in the state. It starts in the Adirondack Mountains. The Mohawk River joins the Hudson near Albany. The Hudson then flows south through the Catskill Mountains, into New York Harbor, and then into the Atlantic Ocean. The Genesee River is one of the few rivers in North America that flow north instead of south. It passes through the Genesee **Gorge**, which is sometimes called the "Grand Canyon of the East."

New York also has many lakes. Two of the Great Lakes—Lake Erie and Lake Ontario—make up part of the border between New York and Canada. Five lakes in the middle of the state are called the Finger Lakes because they are long and narrow, like fingers.

◄ Lake Erie and Lake Ontario are connected by the Niagara River, one of the shortest rivers in the world. The Niagara River tumbles off a cliff that is about 176 feet high, forming one of the world's largest waterfalls, Niagara Falls. This painting of Niagara Falls was done in 1885.

5

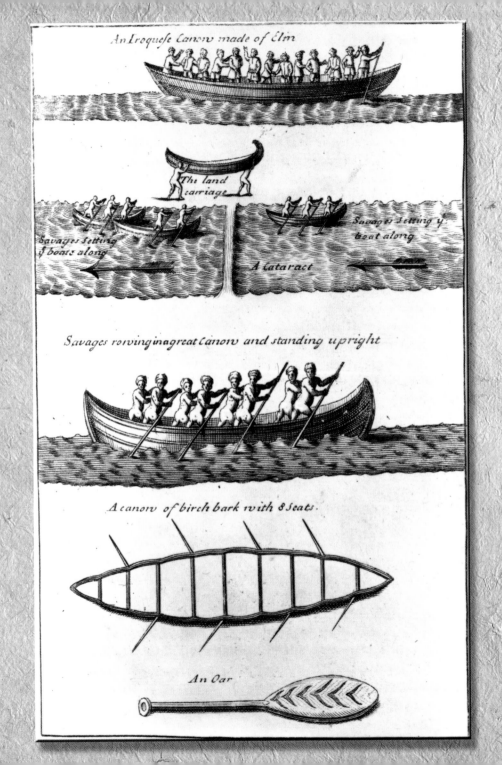

An Iroquese Canow made of Elm

The land carriage

Savages letting the boats along

Savages letting the boat along

A Cataract

Savages rowing in a great Canow and standing upright

A canow of birch bark with 8 Seats.

An Oar

6

Native Americans of New York

Long before Europeans arrived in North America, Native American peoples called the **Algonquian** and **Iroquois** lived in the area that is now New York state. They used the area's many waterways to travel quickly and built strong houses to protect them from the cold winters. The Native Americans built their homes, canoes, tools, and weapons from the wood, bark, and stones they found in the area. They also depended on the area's wildlife for food, clothes, and tools.

The Iroquois planted corn, beans, and squash, which all grew well in the area's climate and rich soil. Once the corn was planted and started growing, the Iroquois planted beans and squash in the same soil. The tall cornstalks supported the bean and squash plants as they grew.

◀ Native Americans in the area that became New York had great respect for nature. They believed that everything in nature had a spirit, from the plants and animals they used for food and shelter, to the wind, water, and Sun. This picture, done about 1703, shows Iroquois people using their canoes and oars, which they made from the bark and wood of trees.

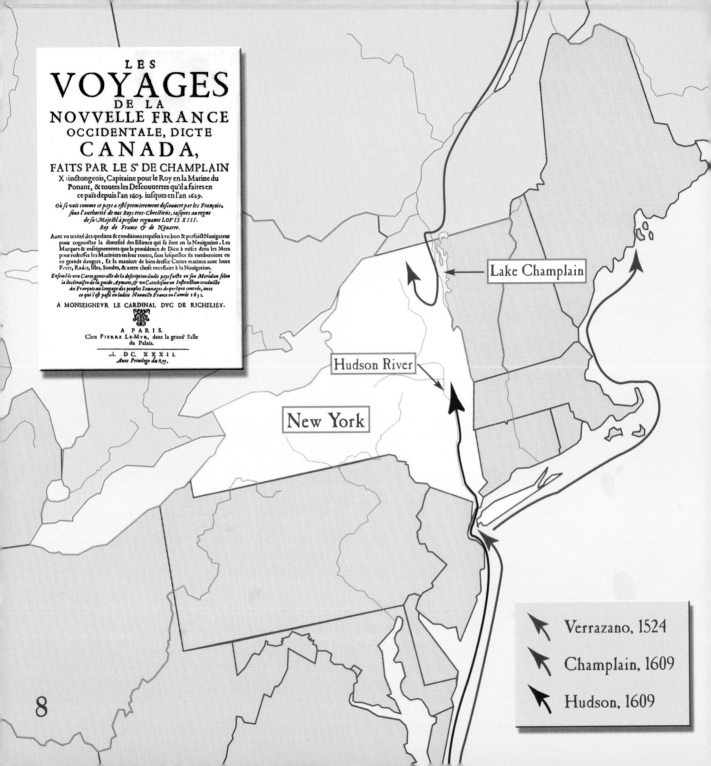

LES
VOYAGES
DE LA
NOVVELLE FRANCE
OCCIDENTALE, DICTE
CANADA,
FAITS PAR LE Sʳ DE CHAMPLAIN

Xainctongeois, Capitaine pour le Roy en la Marine du
Ponant, & toutes les Descouuertes qu'il a faites en
ce païs depuis l'an 1603. iusques en l'an 1629.

Où se voit comme ce pays a esté premierement descouuert par les François,
sous l'authorité de nos Roys tres-Chrestiens, iusques au regne
de sa Majesté à present regnante LOVIS XIII.
Roy de France & de Nauarre.

Auec vn traitté des qualitez & conditions requises à vn bon & parfaict Nauigateur
pour cognoistre la diuersité des Estimes qui se font en la Nauigation, Les
Marques & enseignements que la prouidence de Dieu à mises dans les Mers
pour redresser les Mariniers en leur routte, sans lesquelles ils tomberoient en
ce grandz dangers, Et la maniere de bien dresser Cartes marines auec leurs
Ports, Rades, Isles, Sondes, & autre chose necessaire à la Nauigation.

Ensemble vne Carte generalle de la description dudit pays faitte en son Meridien selon
la declinaison de la guide Aymant, & vn Catechisme ou Instruction traduitte
du François au langage des peuples Sauuages de quelque contrée, auec
ce qui s'est passé en ladite Nouuelle France en l'année 1631.

A MONSEIGNEVR LE CARDINAL DVC DE RICHELIEV.

A PARIS,
Chez PIERRE LE-MVR, dans la grand' Salle
du Palais.

⸱M. DC. XXXII.
Auec Priuilege du Roy.

Lake Champlain

Hudson River

New York

Verrazano, 1524

Champlain, 1609

Hudson, 1609

8

Europeans Explore New York

An Italian named Giovanni da Verrazano was the first European explorer to reach New York. He explored New York Harbor in 1524 and may have sailed up what we now call the Hudson River. Like other explorers who followed, Verrazano wrongly believed that only a narrow strip of land separated him from the Indian Ocean and the riches of Asia.

In 1609, an English explorer named Henry Hudson was hired by the Dutch to search for a new water route to Asia. He entered New York Harbor and sailed north on the river that was later named for him—the Hudson River. Hudson saw that the area had rich soil for planting crops and many **natural resources**, and he claimed it for the Netherlands.

◀ The map shows the routes of Verrazano, Hudson, and a French explorer named Samuel de Champlain. In 1609, Champlain left his fort in present-day Quebec, Canada, and traveled south into New York to explore the area's waterways. During this trip, he found a lake in northern New York that was later named after him—Lake Champlain. The small picture is a page from a book Champlain wrote in 1629 about his voyage.

PART OF EAST NEW JE

Passaic River

Hackensack River

Hudson River

East River

Newark

Newark Bay

Bergen

Elizabethtown

Woodbridge

Ambois

Dover

New Town

STATEN ISLAND

Old Town

Wels

Ferry

West Banks

Oyster Bank

Ship Channel

Fort

New York

Ferry

PART OF LONG ISLAND

Place for winter Kings Ships

Ferry to Staten Island

Gravesend

East Bank

Anchoring Ground

Sand Point

8 fathoms

4 fathoms

Entrance

7 7 9 8 7 18 10 14 14 7 4 19 15 10 8 8 5 4 4 1 3 3 6 7 8 8 12 10 10 6 5 6 5 4 6 6 10 3 5 6 4 5 6 7 1 8 5 4

8 10 10 8 7 8 7 6 5 6 5 6 7 5 6 6 4 5 4 5 7 6 7 5 6 7 3 6

Colonists and New York's Geography

Most early colonial settlements were close to waterways because it was easier and quicker for colonists to travel on the water than by land. Early Dutch and British colonists established settlements on Manhattan Island, along the Hudson River, and in the area that is now the city of Albany. Ships arriving from Europe could dock along the waterways and unload their supplies.

Most Europeans came to the "New World" to make money and did not respect the land like the Native Americans did. After the Europeans arrived, they began changing the **landscape**. They cut down trees and cleared the land for farming. They caught many beavers and other animals for their furs, which were highly valued back in Europe. This reduced the number of animals in the area.

◀ New York Harbor was a valuable bay because it is deep enough for large ships to travel on. The harbor was almost completely surrounded by land, giving ships plenty of places to unload supplies. This map, made in the late 1700s, shows the harbor area. The numbers tell how deep the water is in different places. The lightly shaded areas show where the water is shallow, warning ships not to come too close.

BANKING · BARTERING AND SHIPPING IN NEW AMSTERDAM 1650·

12

From Beaver Furs to Farming

New York's huge supply of wild animals, like beavers, drew many European traders to the area. They could become rich by selling beaver furs to people back in Europe. The European traders gave the Native Americans metal objects, weapons, and cloth in exchange for beaver furs.

Native Americans taught colonists how to hunt and fish, and how to grow foods such as beans, corn, and squash. New York's soil and weather were perfect for farming. As more people arrived or were born in the colonies, farming became more important than beaver furs. Dutch colonists made unfair agreements with Native Americans, trading small amounts of metal tools, cloth, and weapons for thousands of **acres** of land.

◀ New York colonists needed seeds, livestock, and farm tools from Europe. In return, they sent lumber and beaver furs back to Europe. New York's forests grew smaller as more trees were cut down. This picture shows the busy streets of New Amsterdam, where ships picked up furs for Europe and dropped off things for trading. New Amsterdam was later renamed New York City.

13

14   *Broadway - gatan och Rådhuset i New York*

Colonial Buildings and Towns

Dutch settlers had to build houses and forts quickly so they would have shelter from the cold winters and from their enemies. The first homes that New York colonists built were one-room houses made of materials that were easy to find on the land, like logs, bark, and **sod**. Stones were used to make fort walls stronger.

Before the European settlers came to New York, there had been hundreds of miles of forests and untouched land. After the settlers arrived, they began to use more and more materials from New York's land to build farms, barns, and homes like those they had lived in back in Europe. They also used slaves from Africa to help them clear and level the land in order to build towns, changing the countryside forever.

◀ After the British took over New York in 1664, they changed the landscape even more. New York City grew larger as the English built stone and brick houses, shops, taverns, government buildings, churches, and roads. This picture of New York City was made in 1819. The buildings in the picture show the influence of British building styles.

Fighting Over New York

For many years, France and England fought over New York's land and resources. Many battles were fought over the area's waterways, since whoever controlled the waterways would be able to control the land. When the fighting ended in 1763, France had lost most of its land in North America to the English.

Many settlers, including those in New York, grew tired of being ruled by England. They had spent many years farming the land, setting up businesses, and building towns and cities. They had learned how to use the land's resources to take care of their needs. The colonists thought of the colonies as their land, not England's. This led to the American Revolution, a war in which the colonists won their freedom from England.

◀ This painting shows General George Washington marching into New York City after the colonists had won the American Revolution. During the war, Washington sent troops to destroy the villages of Native Americans in New York who had fought for the British. The rich farmland of these Native Americans was given to the colonists.

PAN-AMERICAN

ELECTRIC TOWER
391 FEET HIGH

EXPOSITION: BUFFALO.
May 1st to November 1st 1901

18

New York's Waterways

In the years after the colonies won their freedom from England and became the United States, many new towns were settled between New York City in the southeast and Buffalo, a city on Lake Erie in western New York.

Transportation became important to the quickly growing country. The Erie Canal, finished in 1825, created an all-water route between New York City and Buffalo. In 1897, Buffalo became the first city in the United States to light its streets with electricity. The electricity came from **generators** powered by rushing water from the Niagara River on its way to Niagara Falls. Even today, New York's waterfalls and rivers are some of North America's largest sources of energy.

◄ In 1901, Buffalo hosted the Pan-American Exposition to improve the relationship between North and South America. An exposition is a kind of large public fair. During the Pan-American Exposition, thousands of electric lights lit up the city. Here we see a photograph of the exposition and a poster advertising the exposition's "Electric Tower."

New York's Industry

Along with a large water supply that powers homes, factories, and farms, New York has many other natural resources that play a large role in the state's different businesses. The Adirondack region has large supplies of lead, talc, and zinc, which are used in manufacturing. It also has one of the country's largest supplies of garnets, a stone used to make jewelry. Garnets are even crushed up and used to make sandpaper!

Clay from the Hudson River valley is used to make brick and cement. Stone, gravel, and sand are found throughout the state. These things are all used in construction. Natural gas, found in western New York, is used to provide energy to people throughout New York and other nearby states.

◄ The gas pipeline shown in this photograph from the early 1950s is owned by the New York State Natural Gas Corporation. Gas pipelines like this one bring gas to businesses and homes throughout New York state.

New York Today

Today, there are nearly 19 million people living in New York state. Modern buildings, cities, roads, bridges, and businesses have changed the way New York looks compared to just 100 years ago. New York City has one of the most recognizable **skylines** in all the world. Some cities in New York are facing pollution problems, but New York still has many beautiful natural sights. Because of places like New York City, Lake Placid, Niagara Falls, and the Finger Lakes, **tourism** is one of New York's most important industries.

Glossary

acre (AY-kuhr) An area of land equal to 43,560 square feet.

Algonquian (al-GAHN-kwee-uhn) The name given to several groups of Native Americans in the northeast who spoke Algonquian languages.

generator (JEH-nuh-ray-tuhr) A machine that uses motion to make electricity.

gorge (GORJ) A narrow valley with steep, rocky sides.

Iroquois (EAR-uh-kwoy) The name given to several groups of Native Americans in the northeast who spoke Iroquois languages.

landscape (LAND-skayp) The natural scenery of a particular place.

natural resource (NAH-chuh-ruhl REE-sohrs) Something found on the land or in the water that people can use.

skyline (SKY-line) The outline of buildings against the background of the sky.

sod (SAHD) A layer or section of ground that has grass rooted in it.

tourism (TUHR-ih-zuhm) The business of traveling for pleasure.

transportation (trans-puhr-TAY-shun) The movement of people or goods from one place to another.

Index

C
construction, 21

E
energy, 19, 21
Erie Canal, 19

F
farming, 11, 13, 17
Finger Lakes, 5, 22
forests, 15
furs, 11, 13

H
Hudson River, 5, 9, 11, 21

L
Lake Erie, 5, 19

M
Manhattan Island, 11
manufacturing, 21

N
New York Harbor, 5, 9
Niagara Falls, 19, 22

P
pollution, 22

S
soil, 7, 9, 13

W
waterways, 7, 11, 17

Primary Source List

Cover. Ice bridge below Niagara Falls, winter. Photograph, ca. 1900.
Page 4. *Niagara Falls.* Painting by George Inness, 1885. Now in the Smithsonian American Art Museum, Washington, D.C.
Page 6. Iroquois Indians Canoeing. Engraving from Louis Armand de Lom d'Arce Lahontan's *Nouveaux voyages de Monsieur le baron de Lahontan, dans l'Amerique Septentrionale.* First edition published in 1703.
Page 8 (inset). Title page from Samuel de Champlain's *Voyages de la Nouvelle France.* Written in 1629 and published in Paris in 1632.
Page 10. Nautical chart of New York Bay. Engraving, ca. 1765.
Page 14. *Broadway Street and the City Hall in New York.* From *Bref om de Forenta Staterna, forfattade under en Resa till Amerika aren 1818, 1819, 1820,* by Swedish aristocrat Baron Axel Leonhard Klinckowstrom. Aquatint signed by an artist named Akrell, with an indication that he copied a drawing by Klinckowstrom.
Page 18. Photograph of night view of lighted exhibition buildings along the Esplanade at the Pan-American Exposition, Buffalo, 1901.
Page 18 (inset). Poster of Electric Tower at Pan-American Exposition, Buffalo, 1901.
Page 20. Laying of natural gas pipeline for New York State Natural Gas Corporation. Photograph taken April 13, 1951.

Web Sites

Due to the changing nature of Internet links, The Rosen Publishing Group, Inc. has developed an on-line list of Web sites related to the subjects of this book. This site is updated regularly. Please use this link to access the list:
http://www.rcbmlinks.com/nysh/nylr